# ESSENTIAL ELEMENTS

Audio Access Included

## UKULELE

# EASY STRUMMING SONGS

Chris Kringel, bass/keys/ukulele; Jay Brian Kummer, ukulele
Steve Cohen, harmonica; Mike DeRose, guitar; Jack Dune, drums; Brian Myers, keyboard

## PLAYBACK+
Speed • Pitch • Balance • Loop

To access audio visit:
**www.halleonard.com/mylibrary**

Enter Code
3793-0343-3315-9228

ISBN: 978-1-4950-7217-8

# HAL•LEONARD

Visit Hal Leonard Online at
**www.halleonard.com**

Contact Us:
**Hal Leonard**
7777 West Bluemound Road
Milwaukee, WI 53213
Email: info@halleonard.com

In Europe contact:
**Hal Leonard Europe Limited**
Distribution Centre, Newmarket Road
Bury St Edmunds, Suffolk, IP33 3YB
Email: info@halleonardeurope.com

In Australia contact:
**Hal Leonard Australia Pty. Ltd.**
4 Lentara Court
Cheltenham, Victoria, 3192 Australia
Email: info@halleonard.com.au

# STRUM PATTERNS

These strum patterns are referred to by number at the beginning of each song.
Use the suggested strumming rhythm throughout the piece unless otherwise indicated in the music.
The symbols ⊓ and ∨ refer to down and up strokes, respectively.

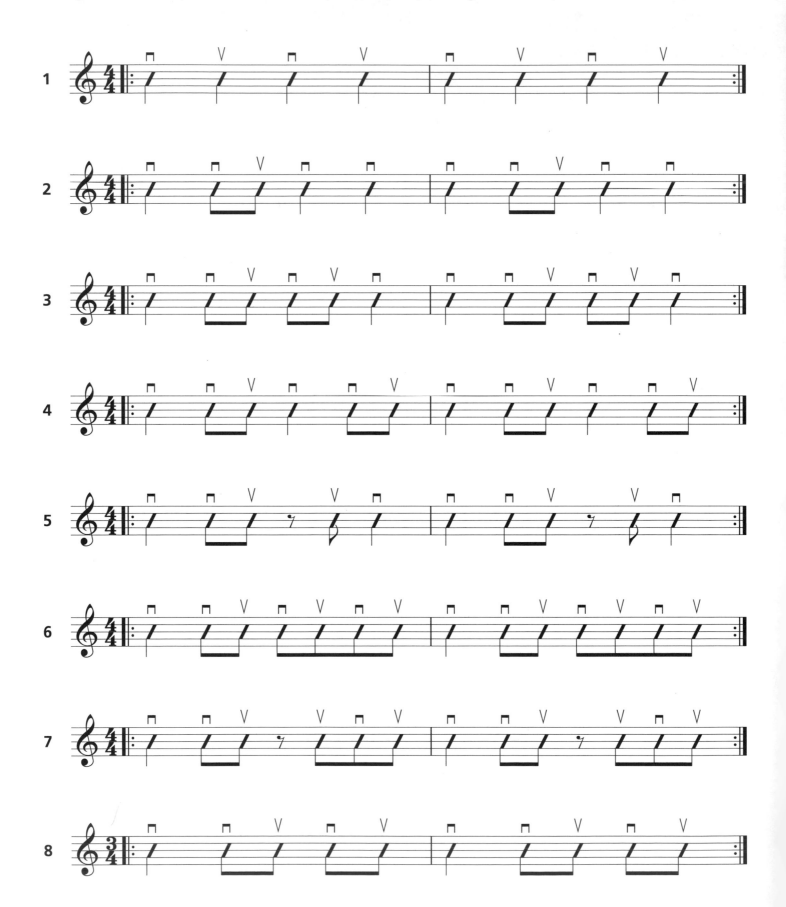

# DAY-O
## (The Banana Boat Song)

Words and Music by Irving Burgie and William Attaway

**Strum Pattern: 6**

**Intro**
**Moderate Calypso**

1. Work all night _ on a drink of rum. _ Day-light come _ and me wan' go home. Stack ba-nan-a till dc morn-ing come. _ Day-light come _ and me wan' go home.

**Bridge**

Come, Mis-ter Tal-ly Man, tal-ly me ba-nan-a. Day-light come _ and me wan' go home.

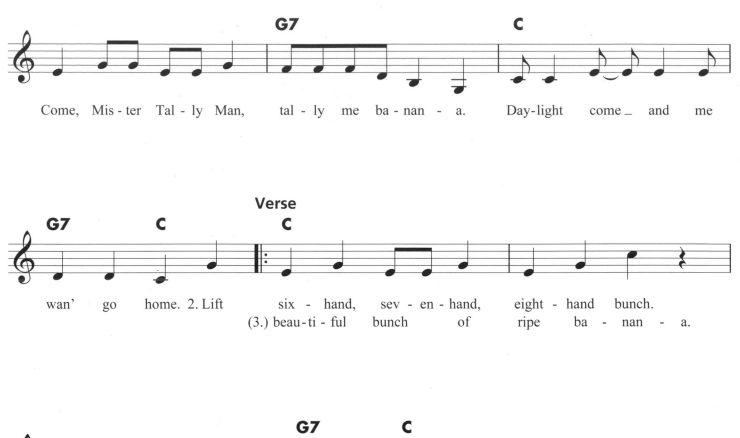

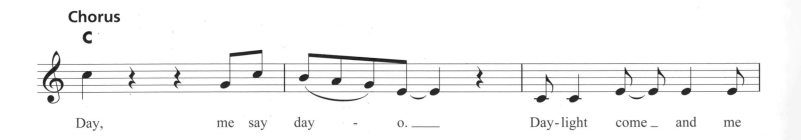

# IRIS

### from the Motion Picture CITY OF ANGELS
#### Words and Music by John Rzeznik

**1.**

Am              G             F

_____ want to go _____ home right now.        2. And all _____

_____ want to miss _____ you to -

**2.**

**Chorus**

F                         Am             G

night.       And I _____ don't want the world _____ to

F                       Am           G

see me      'cause I _____ don't _____ think that they'd _____ un - der -

F                       Am           G

stand.       When ev - 'ry - thing's _ made to be _____ bro -

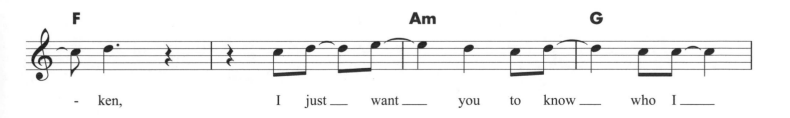

F                       Am           G

- ken,       I just _____ want _____ you to know _____ who I _____

am.

3. And you can't ___ fight the tears ___ that ain't com-

- ing, ___ or the ___ mo - ment of truth ___ in your ___

lies. When ev - 'ry - thing feels ___ like the mov-

- ies, yeah, you ___ bleed ___ just to know ___ you're a-

**Chorus**

live. And I ___ don't want the world ___ to see ___

___ me 'cause I ___ don't ___ think that they'd ___ un - der-

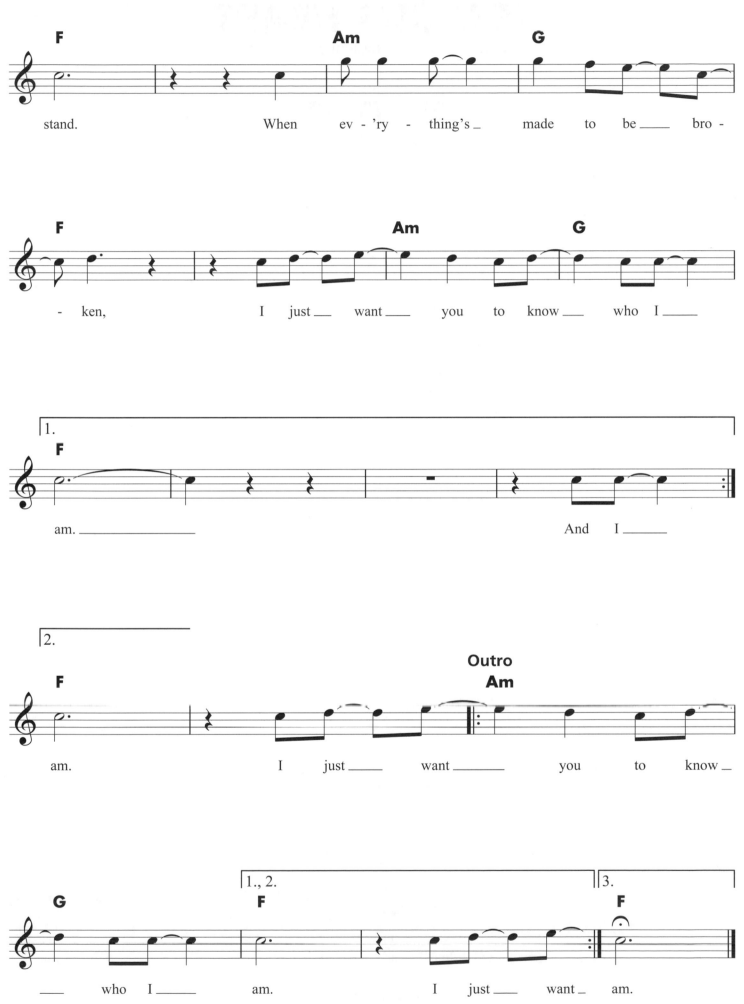

# JEALOUS HEART

Words and Music by Jenny Lou Carson

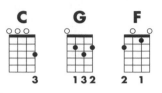

**Strum Pattern: 3**

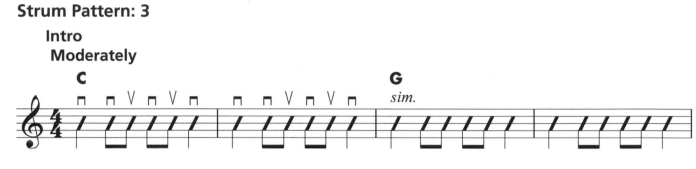

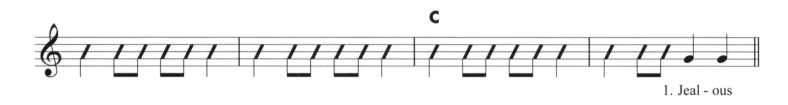

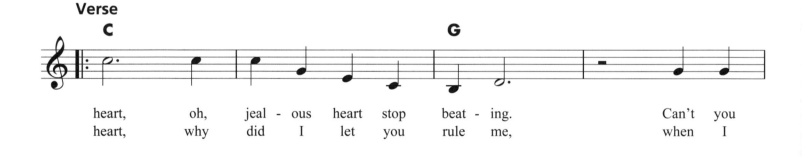

heart,  oh,  jeal - ous  heart  stop  beat - ing.  Can't  you
heart,  why  did  I  let  you  rule  me,  when  I

see  the  dam - age  you  have  done?  You  have
knew  the  end  would  bring  me  pain?  Now  she's

driv - en  her  a - way  for - ev - er.  Jeal - ous
gone,  she's  gone  and  found  an - oth - er.  Oh,  I'll

heart, now I'm the lone - ly one. I was
nev - er see my love a - gain. Man - y

**Chorus**

part of ev - 'ry - thing she planned for, and I
times I trust - ed you to guide me, but your

know she loved me at the start. Now she
guid - ing on - ly brought me tears. Why, oh,

hates the sight of all I stand for, all be -
why must I have you in - side me, jeal - ous

cause of you, oh, jeal - ous heart.
heart, for all my lone - ly years?

**Solo**

**C**

**G**

1. 2.

**C**

2. Jeal-ous    Through the

**Chorus**

**F**                                            **C**

years,    her   mem - o - ry   will   haunt   me,                    e - ven

**G**                                            **C**

though    we're   man - y   miles   a - part.                    It's   so

**F**                                            **C**

hard    to   know   she'll   nev - er   want   me,                    'cause   she

**G**                                            **C**

heard    your   beat - ing   jeal - ous   heart. _____

# PEPPERMINT TWIST

Words and Music by Joseph DiNicola and Henry Glover

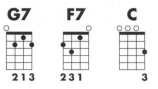

**Strum Pattern: 3**

**Intro**
**Moderately fast**

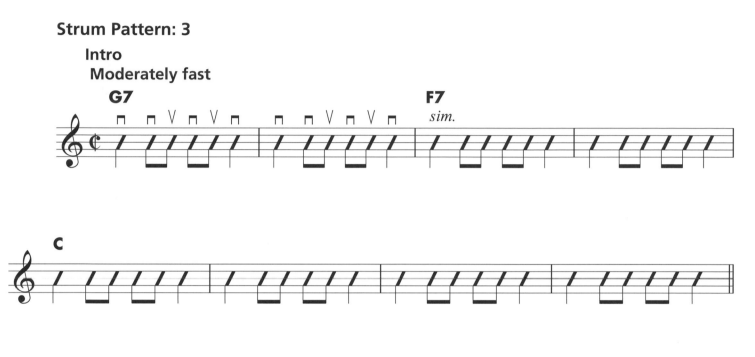

**Verse**

1. Got a new dance and it goes like this.
   The name of this dance is the Pep-per-mint Twist.
   You'll like _____ it like this, _____ the Pep-per-mint Twist. _____

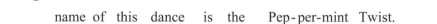

**Verse**

2. Meet me, ba - by, on For - ty - fifth Street

where the Pep - per - mint Twist - ers meet. _ You'll

learn ____ to do this, ___ the Pep - per - mint Twist. _

**Chorus**

'Round and 'round, up and down, 'round and

'round, up and down. It's 'round and 'round and

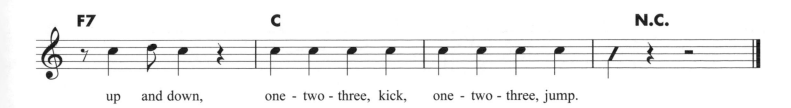

up and down, one - two - three, kick, one - two - three, jump.

# LOSING MY RELIGION

Words and Music by William Berry, Peter Buck, Michael Mills and Michael Stipe

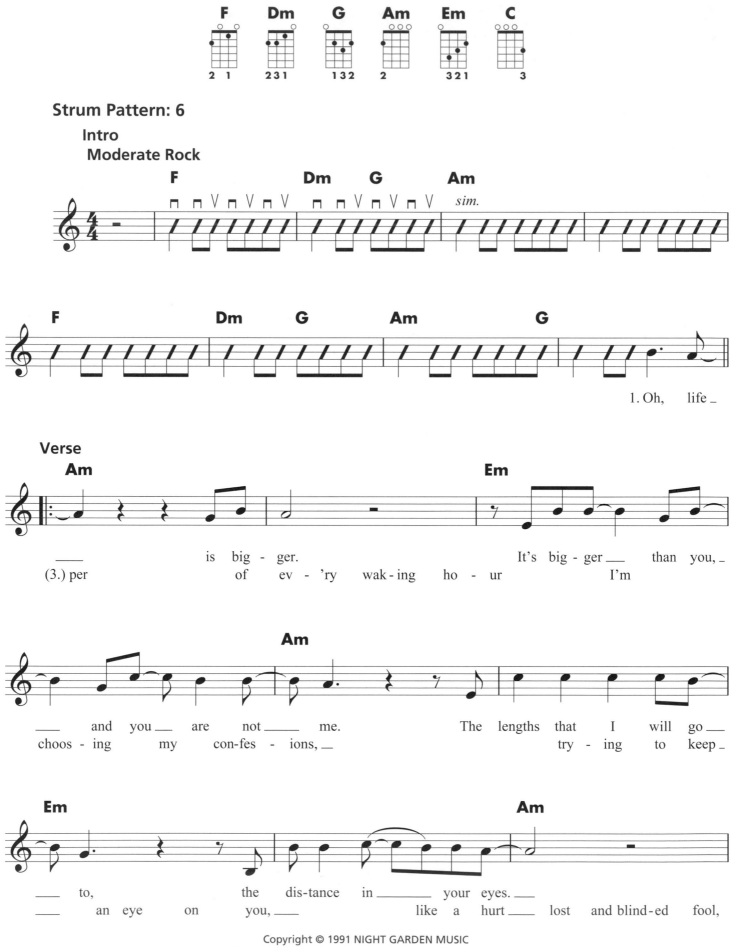

**Chorus**

ing.      I thought that I heard you sing. \_\_\_      I

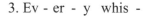

think I thought I saw you try. \_\_\_      3. Ev - er - y whis -

**Interlude**

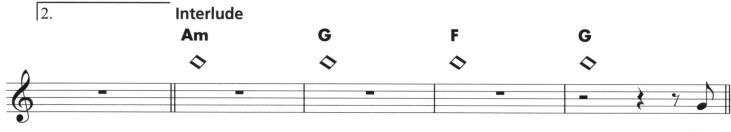

But

**Bridge**

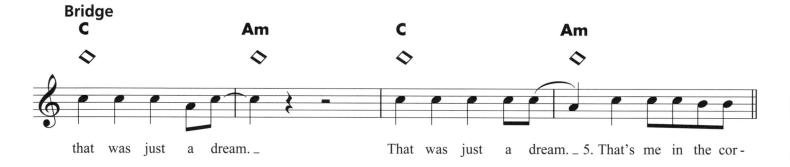

that was just a dream. \_      That was just a dream. \_ 5. That's me in the cor -

**Verse**

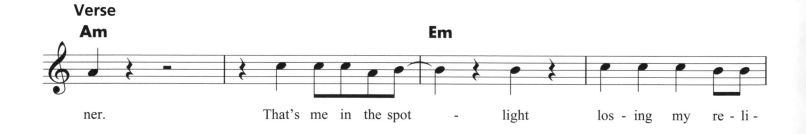

ner.      That's me in the spot - light los - ing my re - li -

gion,      try - ing to keep \_\_ up \_\_ with you, \_\_ and I don't \_

# ON THE ROAD AGAIN

Words and Music by Willie Nelson

**Strum Pattern: 1**

**Intro**
**Moderately fast**

1. On the

**Verse**

road a - gain.          Just can't    wait  to get    on   the
road a - gain,          go - in'     plac - es    that  I've

road a - gain.          The  life  I  love  is  mak - in'
nev - er  been,                    see - in' things _ that  I  may

mu - sic  with  my  friends, __          and    I  can't  wait  to  get
nev - er  see  a - gain, ____          and    I  can't  wait  to  get

on  the  road _ a - gain. __          2. On  the
on  the  road _ a - gain. __          On  the

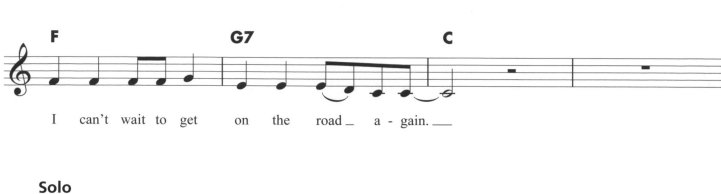

I can't wait to get on the road _ a - gain. _

**Solo**

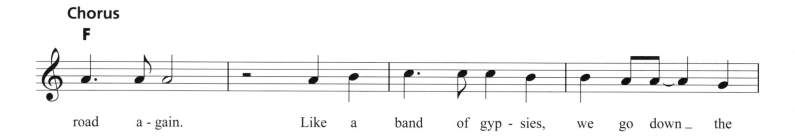

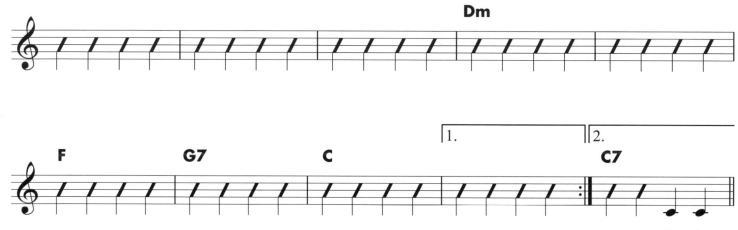

On the

**Chorus**

road a - gain. Like a band of gyp - sies, we go down _ the

high - way. We're the best of friends, in -

sist - ing that the world keep turn - ing our way, and

# PAINT IT, BLACK

Words and Music by Mick Jagger and Keith Richards

**5.**  **1.-3.**

**Interlude**
**A**  **Dm**  **A7**

Mm.

**4.**

**Bridge**
**Dm**

I wan-na see your face  paint-ed  black,

**A7**  **Dm**

black as night, _  black as coal. _  I wan-na see the sun

**A7**

blot-ted  out  from the sky.  I wan-na see it

**Dm**  **A7**

paint-ed, paint-ed,  paint-ed,  paint-ed black,  yeah. _

**Outro**  *Repeat and fade*
**Dm**  **A7**

Mm.

*Additional Lyrics*

3. I look inside myself and see my heart is black.
I see my red door, I must have it painted black.
Maybe then I'll fade away and not have to face the facts.
It's not easy facing up when your whole world is black.

4. No more will my green sea go turn a deeper blue.
I could not foresee this thing happening to you.
If I look hard enough into the setting sun,
My love will laugh with me before the morning comes.

# SUNDOWN

Words and Music by Gordon Lightfoot

F    C7    Bb    Eb

2 1       1    3211    2 3 1

**Strum Pattern: 7**

**Intro**
**Moderately**

F

*sim.*

|1.

|2.

**Verse**
F

1. I can see her ly-ing back in her sat-in dress __ in a
look-ing like a queen in a sail-or's dream, __ and she
3., 4. *See additional lyrics*

C7                                    F          **Chorus**    F

room where you do __ what you don't con-fess. __    Sun-down, you
don't al-ways say __ what she real-ly means. __    Some-times I

Bb                              Eb                            F

bet-ter take care __ if I find you been creep-in' 'round __ my back stairs. __
think it's a shame __ when I get feel-ing bet-ter, when I'm feel-ing no pain. __

*Additional Lyrics*

3. I can picture ev'ry move that a man could make.
   Getting lost in her loving is your first mistake.
   Sundown, you better take care if I find you been creepin' 'round my back stairs.
   Sometimes I think it's a sin when I feel like I'm winning when I'm losing again.

4. I can see her looking fast in her faded jeans.
   She's a hard-loving woman, got me feeling mean.
   Sometimes I think it's a shame when I get feeling better, when I'm feeling no pain.
   Sundown, you better take care if I find you been creepin' 'round my back stairs.

# TIME FOR ME TO FLY

Words and Music by Kevin Cronin

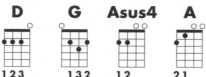

**Strum Pattern: 3**

**Intro**
**Moderately fast**

**Verse**

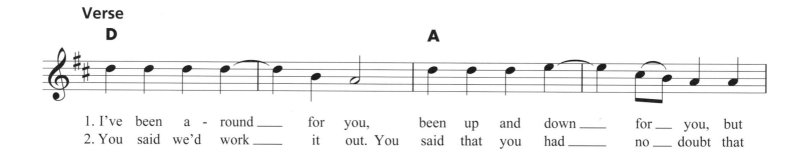

1. I've been a - round ____ for you, been up and down ____ for ____ you, but
2. You said we'd work ____ it out. You said that you had ____ no ____ doubt that

I just can't get an - y re - lief. ____           I've
deep down we were real - ly in love. ____           But

swal - lowed my pride ____ for you, lived and lied ____ for ____ you, but
I'm tired of hold - ing on to a feel - ing I know ____ is ____ gone. I

you still make me feel like a thief. _____ You got me
do be-lieve that I've had e-nough. _____ I've had e-

steal-in' your love _____ a-way 'cause you nev-er give _____ it;
nough of the false - ness of a worn-out re-la - tion,  e-

peel-in' the years _____ a-way, and we can't re-live _____ it. }
nough of the jeal - ous-y and the in-tol-er-a - tion.)

I make you laugh, _____ and _ you make me cry. _____

I be-lieve it's time _____ for me _ to fly. _____

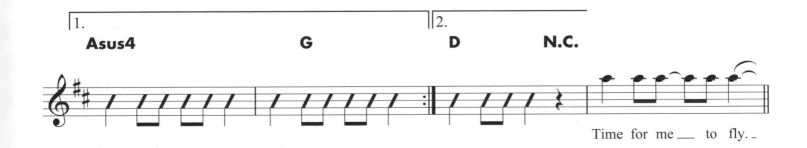

Time for me _ to fly. _

**Chorus**

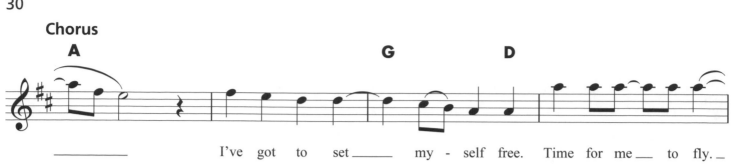

I've got to set ____ my - self free. Time for me __ to fly. __

That's just how it's got to ____ be. _____

I know it hurts to say __ good - bye, ____ but it's time for me __ to fly. __

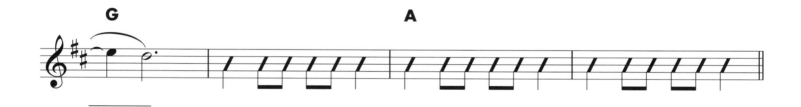

_____

**Interlude**

**Asus4**

**D**                                       **N.C.**

Time for me __ to fly. __

**Chorus**

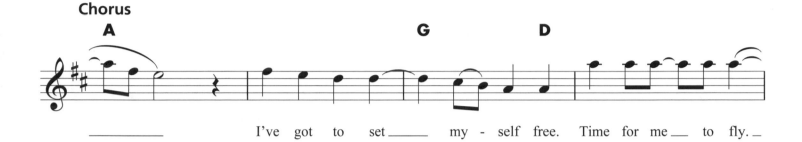

**A**                       **G**         **D**

_____ I've got to set ____ my-self free. Time for me __ to fly. __

**A**                       **G**         **D**

_____ That's just how it's got to ____ be. _____

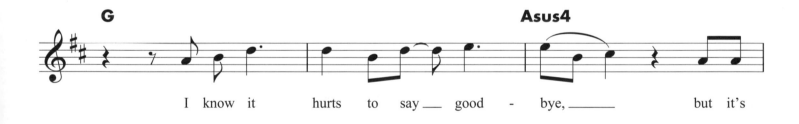

**G**                             **Asus4**

I know it hurts to say __ good - bye, _____ but it's

                      **G**                             **A**

time for me __ to fly. _____ It's

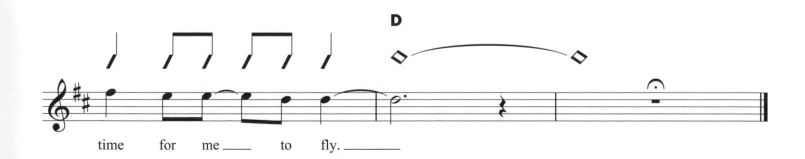

                                      **D**

time for me __ to fly. _____

# WALK OF LIFE

Words and Music by Mark Knopfler

**Chorus**

**Interlude**

**Outro**

*Repeat and fade*

# WITH OR WITHOUT YOU

Words and Music by U2

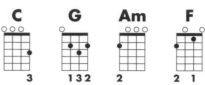

**Strum Pattern: 4**

**Intro**
**Moderately**

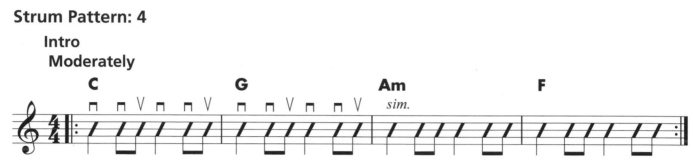

**Verse**

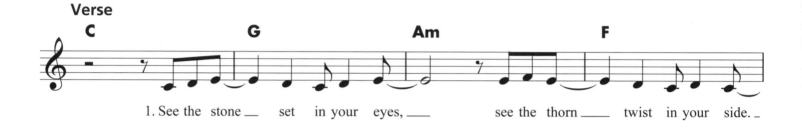

1. See the stone __ set in your eyes, __ see the thorn __ twist in your side. __

__ I'll wait __ for you. __

**Verse**

2. Sleight of hand __ and twist of fate, __ on a bed of nails __
3. Through the storm __ we reach the shore. __ You give it all, __

__ she makes me wait, __ and I wait __ with - out __
__ but I want more, __ and I'm wait - ing for

with or with - out _____ you. _____

**Interlude**

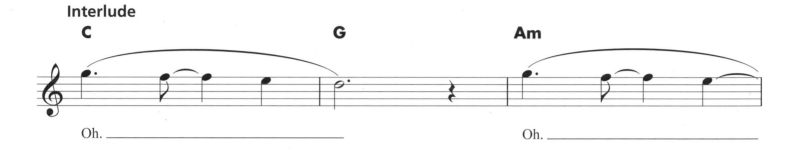

Oh. _____ Oh. _____

_____ Oh, _____ oh, oh. __

**Outro-Chorus**

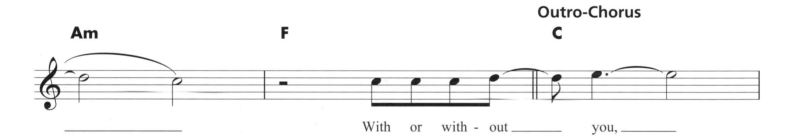

_____ With or with - out _____ you, _____

with or with - out you, __ uh - huh. _____ I can't live __

___ with or with - out _____ you,

with or with - out you. ____

# WONDERFUL TONIGHT

Words and Music by Eric Clapton

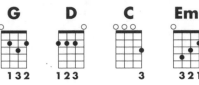

**Strum Pattern: 2**

1. It's late in the eve - ning; ___ she's won-d'ring what clothes ___
2. We go to a par - ty, ___ ev - 'ry - one turns ___

___ to wear. ___ She puts on her make - up ___
___ to see ___ this beau - ti - ful la - dy ___

and brush-es her long, ___ blonde hair. ___ And then she asks ___
is walk-ing a - round ___ with me. ___ And then she asks ___

___ me, ___ "Do I look al - right?" ___ And I say,
___ me, ___ "Do you feel al - right?" ___ And I say,

**D**       **C**       **D**

___ now, _____ and I've got an ach - ing head.

**G**       **D**       **C**

So I give her the car ___ keys, ___ and she helps me to

**D**       **C**       **D**

bed. And then I tell ___ her, ___

**G**    **D**    **Em**       **C**

as I turn out the light, ___ I say, "My dar - ling, you are

**D**       **G**   **D**   **Em**   **D**

won - der - ful ___ to - night. ___ Oh, my

**C**       **D**       **G**

dar - ling, you are won - der - ful ___ to - night." ___

**Outro**

|1.| |2.|

**D**    **C**    **D**    **G**       **G**

*2nd time, rit.*